tidal wave

kofi antwi

Tidal Wave $10
Kofi Antwi
ISBN 978-1-944252-35-9
Kattywompus Press

Publisher's Position Statement
on the Value of Poetry Arts

This chapbook is a work of fine art from the poet

Kofi Antwi

whose work you support for a few cents per page.   You are
not buying paper and printer's ink by weight.   You selected
language art that took as long to create as paintings or other
fine art. On behalf of a large community of contemporary poets,
this poet in particular, independent and small press publishing,
and Kattywompus Press, thank you for supporting this project.

KATTYWOMPUS PRESS

www.kattywompuspress.com
22 Line St. Unit E
Somerville, MA 02143

Acknowledgments

BMCC Writers Guild: all hail the city of doom
Kalahari Review: an ode to agony
Best of Africa: when you arrive at your new home
Rigorous: gray space and matter, byproduct
Writers With Attitude: sundays
Rise Up: vintage
Great Weather For Media: tidal wave

~

where there is love it will manifest in abundance.
to my family — Alicia and Kofi Ali Antwi, thank you.

a special gratitude to my family, friends, and colleagues
that offered light to my poetry.

thank you to the Writers Foundry
and Cave Canem for providing space and
literary fellowships.

in closing, I would like to acknowledge the readers of
Tidal Wave.

thank you Santrokofi, Ghana, the city of Accra,
Brooklyn, Upstate New York, and
Staten Island

Contents

out of wreckage

awaken – morning star,
once beloved brother,
submerged in flagellant

thoughts –

buried dead or alive,
bounties
rise and mark–stock,

a belated shower
of roses – an unholy
atrocity,

the undertaker pivots,
reclaim faulty grounds.
april, will you depart

the great valley of
mourning and evade
a fading interlude

.

Gray Space & Matter – noun. an ill-defined situation or field not readily conforming to category or and an existing set of rules. some equate its shade through area or matter. the only hue – consist of process/ congested thoughts. we never tripped over selected diction   or placement/ rather spoke peace, then chuck deuces/   rather it be free will / or a universe relegated to fraudulent tales/ our communities are regulated / where limits are placed/   the mind seeks food for thought less?

light years, at bay

and bloom. what is preordained – pardons a
sea or regrets, an interval.

enter the 36 chambers   perplexed,
comprehension fleets or is absent;

spirit is questioned, solace riddles a poet,
love is love, or war – bargains power.

tide submerges our faults, we
dance, toiled the fruit –

&   bared witness,
november (the 21st day). a crescent

smile suspends   perpetual
sky,   space prolong fixtures

before men feast   we
prepared a table, in riches –

of laughter & joy, there is an art
in poetry and assembling the gods

silver lakes

it was as if evening
broke day, bread, *oh*

Christ, and things I hate
to confess, dare to love –

solitude, and summer's
overflow of sundance

yellow leaves forewarn winter's
rush. A *tidal wave* submerges,

allegory you must defend,
chords elevates a quadrant,

the shore of our island,
I – adore, april ascends

a fling with Ms. Jazz June

allow I to arouse your heart, drifting
before the fading moon, let
it not be our last, We

dance to your favorite tune
sing fate of blues
Ms. Brooks *Jazz June*

our spring nights longing
you, may showers, drunken tongue. We
cherish you

sundays

the harbor is burdened land, tampered
sea – a ripple in the
current halts it's viability.

at bay we, mourn our past, balance
tomorrow's deficiencies,
dashes of mint dove

dissolve on brown skin, we
peak past familiar
banks – bush avenue, harbored

roads, our terrace borders
the island. a subtle smile
raises your brows,

we are confined to
seats – a graceful dance
between brisk breath

dissipate. observant of
commuters – they, like us,
stultify their journey

light – noun. the natural agent that stimulates sight. in physics, the term light sometimes refers to electromagnetic radiation of any wavelength, whether visible or not. what was once slumber shines profusely, an account of fluorescent discoveries, as when a partner leads with love, sheds truth in pursuit to combat falsealilty, darkness – ignites a cryptic cyph, it's counterpart imparts shade, casting doubt. some bodies and or matter must travel at its own speed. like when one buries the past and walks with a lighter load, a burden is forgiven. a body is grieved.

a letter from NOLA (2018)

first, one cracks then penetrates
ruby shells, slings – lyrical dope.

outcaste artist parleys,
levies mourn hope,

poverty continues to flood. an
outer crust remains tarnished, *baby*

it's neighbor jaded as
distant memory,

array of pastel buildings
recount catastrophic events,

thumbing her pain
time recoils history

symphony of horns escape –
forgotten lips, *here they come*

marching, allusive spunk,
who dat, natives of common land.

cemeteries float – past poverty
line, tourist lounge within French

quarters' salivating over
Café Du Monde beignets

vintage

orange can't fathom what **black** is, — *I'm*
rooting for everyone black to appraise their skin,
the dystopian perpetuates, rivers forge mind,
matter to pieces of fragments, but I'm blacker
than black, or blue phi. kids are dancing and shuffling
but – I don't have a buck to give no more, or less – I
give   what has been taken,   next stop *two fiff* and
everything is depleted.

discovery

mankind leaps past galaxies – an odyssey
distance – self and or mind, yet again has found
home, delivering although absent – indifferent

attest gravity's relations, matter and time
what is today's mathematics? physics;
knowledge of self, bare one's burden –

adherences, a drunk kin we grow to detest
     judge; calculated space – it takes distance,
to apply data on earth, yet one must cope

with reality, board cosmic flights, silence;
 – entrap syllables, release oxygen,
there seems to be an everlasting

tug – of war between toxins and
memory, both entering never washing –
     away one's pain

Darkness – *adj.* the partial or total absence of light.
wickedness or evil. its pitch arises death out of life, probing
fields of thorns, before dissolving by coast lines, embrace
obscurity's shadows. as time and rivers part matter. willingly
you concede, it seeps as the tide accumulates
when one descends into purgatory
objectively speaking -- limited spaces are shades of bodies
like private clubs in retrospect, champagne dreams never remise

an ode to agony

community, kin,

lives that matter

> *black & blues*

cold as ice,

souls –

displaced;

a perpetual

                    atrocity,

families offer: cognac,

stale hugs

despair

colorful roman —

candles,

the core

reveals; a ghetto

homage..

all hail the city of doom

downtown: we bypass ditches, potholes,
              engraved – a slender terrace, clench
              stenches of grinded coffee
              white boys and girls, squander
              forefather's commandments,
              construction workers squat
              aimlessly on dainty street curbs, laughing

bay street: pimps hustle work, selling perpetual
              sins – we, condemn & flood corners,
              we are all living in our last days
              the unholy man – rattles his cup,
              exposes hardships to
              privileged.   drunk or not,

north shore: police officers unlawfully stop
              and frisk, bash skulls
              unruly clergy men push dope – strike
              their wives, lie and cover it up.
              all hail the city of doom – an island
              constructed for not us, but choke outs,
              and the greater America, that doesn't include us

water

moments before the baptism

offerings, without ceilings,
      or droughts. a core dissolves,
the down pour of tenants –
      coltrane
      we cherish blessings
      bow our heads
      and face a love supreme

– ice precipitates,
      our hands speak for us,
& smack, name of grace.
      ivory coast
      skin, concealed; exodus
      verse, snares
      of french kisses

tidal wave

*an unusually high sea wave that is triggered especially by
an earthquake. an unusual rise of water alongshore due to
strong winds. something overwhelming epically in quantity
or size.*

a ripple undercuts time, migrates bodies,
an overturn, deposits plights of war and or
love, withdrawn; the ghetto poet's balcony –
honest brother's doctrine, *it was written* in
blood, a vivid vortex redirects subjects,
erosion precipitates – a path clears and mirrors
synergy, currents heave one last wish; yesterdays
affairs remain prevalent, death capsulate time.
electric tendency surges through fazes,
contemporary art remains nameless, as air
stifles; time is ominous. its dialect   at bay; we — tease possibilities
and placement, sell out in functions, buck, buck,
buck and pass, i am awaiting *the chronic,*
to hit our shores, sea – speak our native
tongue of Twi. stones, rebels, lay
beneath us —

                                        must pass, too

birth into a nation

displace neighbors' bodies,
build walls and burn bridges.

a herald of chants commence –
celebrate birth, summon the servants

to provide care, fireworks
eradicate – a fallen sky.

from conception   we,
sing a futile tune –

and recollect tales,
a border divides

north from south, field
has thicken between

prehistoric knowledge &
common wealth

when you arrive at your new home

made men politic & and strut government halls,
and disrupt the premise of logic, a conundrum will strike,,
judge; and juries pander, parties benefit, civil
servants claim diplomatic immunity, citizens
willingly bleed—ivory stars, lines separate
streaks of blood, streaming pacific blue, but
life remains pragmatic, we rush to comities
secured by trust funds we are unable to reap.
righteous politicians swears, protect land blessed
upon forefather's servants, city halls of broad
concrete streets – uphold sovereignty you seek,
bloodhound dogs nip at unrested feet

recollections of the Gold Coast

I am we, the dream
>resurrected

>>the case trial and verdict
>>guilty of all counts

fear, religion, frightens
>sapped souls

while faith breeds eternal forgiveness

>>i am we, a tired fist peering through night
>>capturing fearless panthers –
>>piercing roars

>>a movement, off spring – to kin
>>united we stand but man clings
>>on fears, illusion,
>>separating mankind from humanity

I am we, Cape Coast where tender hands
were battered into dusty stones
i am we